Raintree is an imprint of Capstone Global Library
Limited, a company incorporated in England and
Wales having its registered office at 7 Pilgrim
Street, London, EC4V 6LB - Registered company
number: 6695582

First published by Raintree in 2014
The moral rights of the proprietor have been
asserted.

Originally published by DC Comics in the U.S. in
single magazine form as The Batman Strikes! #5.
Copyright © 2014 DC Comics. All Rights Reserved.

Ashley C. Andersen Zantop *Publisher*
Michael Dahl *Editorial Director*
Sean Tulien *Editor*
Heather Kindseth *Creative Director*
Bob Lentz and Hilary Wacholz *Designers*
Tori Abraham *Production Specialist*

DC COMICS
Joan Hilty & Harvey Richards *Original U.S. Editors*
Jeff Matsuda & Dave McCaig *Cover Artists*

ISBN 978 1 406 28568 0

Printed in China.
18 17 16 15
10 9 8 7 6 5 4 3 2

British Library Cataloguing in Publication Data
A full catalogue record for this book is available
from the British Library.

SCARFACE IS GONNA GO BOOM!

BILL MATHENY ....WRITER

CHRISTOPHER JONES ....PENCILLER

TERRY BEATTY...INKER

HEROIC AGE...COLOURIST

PAT BROSSEAU ....LETTERER

BATMAN CREATED BY
BOB KANE

DEADLY PARTNER

BILL MATHENY
WRITER

CHRISTOPHER
JONES
PENCILLER

TERRY BEATTY
INKER

PHIL BALSMAN
LETTERER

HEROIC AGE
COLORIST

NACHIE CASTRO
EDITOR

BATMAN
CREATED BY
BOB KANE

I TOLD YOU BOYS, I GOT *NOTHING* LEFT!

I'M ALREADY TAPPED OUT FROM THE OTHER COLLECTORS!

OTHER COLLECTORS? *WHO? MR. SCARFACE* PROVIDES BUSINESS INSURANCE IN GOTHAM.

YOU KNOW THE ARRANGEMENT. YOU PAY MR. SCARFACE OR BAD THINGS CAN HAPPEN...

IF YOU BR
YOU BOUG

LIKE TO THIS LEFT ARM. IF YOU AIN'T CAREFUL, IT MIGHT GET BROKEN!

LISTEN, NO DISRESPECT TO MR. SCARFACE, BUT THE OTHER GUY...

...IS *MR. THORNE,* AND HE SERVES THE LOCAL BUSINESS COMMUNITY.

SO YOU TWO CAN WALK OUT OF HERE NOW OR RIDE IN AN *AMBULANCE!* IT DOESN'T MATTER TO...

EVENING, *DETECTIVE BENNET, DETECTIVE YIN.* YOU'RE JUST IN TIME FOR THE PARTY.

GLAD TO HEAR IT. WE HEARD THE CALL AND DECIDED TO STOP BY FOR CHIPS AND DIP.

CUTE.

WHAT CAN I SAY? I'M A *PARTY ANIMAL.*

WHUMDP

YOU'VE GOT TO ADMIT, THE MAN HAS STYLE.

"THE MAN" IS A *VIGILANTE,* AND THAT'S AGAINST THE LAW.

DET 027

8

HA HA *HA!* BOXERS. YOU'RE *FUNNY,* MR. SCARFACE!

BOSS, *IT'S THORNE!* HE WANTS TO TALK WITH YOU.

THORNE?! HOW'D THAT *PINHEAD* GET MY NUMBER? IT'S SUPPOSED TO BE UNLISTED!

CAN I HELP YOU, MR. THORNE?

GIVE *ME* THE PHONE, DUMMY! THIS IS BETWEEN THORNE AND ME!

THORNE? SCARFACE HERE. STICK YOUR *NOSE* IN MY BUSINESS AGAIN AND I'LL *SLAP* IT OFF!

JUST LIKE YOU DID THE BATMAN, HUH? EVERYBODY'S STILL LAUGHING ABOUT HOW HE *PUNKED* THE MIGHTY SCARFACE!

BATMAN? PUNK *ME?* HE GOT *LUCKY,* THORNE.

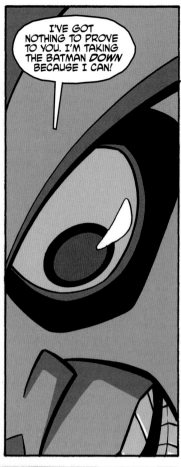

NICE MOVE, *ETHAN.* YOU'VE STILL GOT PLENTY OF HOPS.

I WISH. PLUS, IT'S NOT *MY* HOUSE, IT'S *YOUR* HOUSE. I'M JUST HERE FOR THE HOOPS AND THE HOT WINGS.

SOMETIMES I FEEL LIKE YOU'VE SPENT TWENTY YEARS KICKING MY BUTT ON THE COURT.

ALMOST. WE MET A FEW MONTHS AFTER *YOUR PARENTS...*

HEY, I'M SORRY ABOUT THAT, MAN. I KNOW IT TOOK YOU A LOT OF YEARS TO RECOVER FROM WHAT HAPPENED.

I NEVER DID. AND DON'T SWEAT IT.

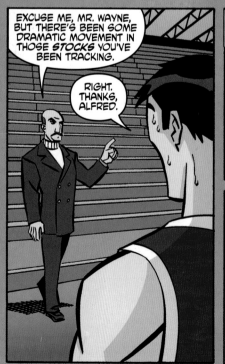

EXCUSE ME, MR. WAYNE, BUT THERE'S BEEN SOME DRAMATIC MOVEMENT IN THOSE *STOCKS* YOU'VE BEEN TRACKING.

RIGHT. THANKS, ALFRED.

TRACKING STOCKS? IT'S 6:00 AT NIGHT.

THREE WORDS: AFTER-HOURS MARKET.

LOOKS LIKE I'M ABOUT TO GET BUSY, TOO. DUTY AND MY DEDICATED PARTNER CALLS. LATER, BRUCE.

BE SAFE, ETHAN.

BEEP BEEP

12

ACCORDING TO THE *SCANNER MESSAGES* YOU HEARD, SCARFACE AND THORNE ARE LEANING HARD ON SHOP OWNERS.

MOSTLY SCARFACE. AND MOSTLY ON GOTHAM'S WEST SIDE.

WHICH BRINGS UP A TROUBLING QUESTION, SIR...

...ISN'T THE VOLUME AND PATTERN OF TONIGHT'S CRIMES RATHER *OBVIOUS?*

TRUE, BUT WE ARE TALKING ABOUT A MAN WHO TAKES ORDERS FROM HIS OWN *VENTRILOQUIST'S DUMMY.*

TOUCHÉ.

WHAT... IS... THIS... THING?

YOUR *PARTNER*, BATS. NOW HOLD ME UPRIGHT, OR NEXT TIME MY *INTERNAL GYRO THINGY* CRANKS UP THE VOLTAGE!

YOU GOT *TEN MINUTES*, BATMAN. THEN IT *EXPLODES*, TAKING YOU AND A CITY BLOCK ALONG FOR THE RIDE!

PFAFF

I'VE GOT TO GET AWAY... THINK...

WHAT DO YA KNOW? THE BAT'S TAKIN' ME CRUISING!

HE'S GETTING AWAY, MR. SCARFACE!

RELAX, DUMMY. THE BAT'S LIVING ON BORROWED TIME. AND IF HE TRIES REMOVING HIS PARTNER...

...BATMAN GOES *SPLAT*, MAN!

GOOD HEAVENS, SIR! DON'T TELL ME THAT YOU'VE DECIDED TO JOIN THE *CARNIVAL*.

18

CREATORS

BILL MATHENY WRITER

Along with comics such as THE BATMAN STRIKES, Bill Matheny has written for TV series including KRYPTO THE SUPERDOG, WHERE'S WALDO, A PUP NAMED SCOOBY-DOO, and many others.

CHRISTOPHER JONES PENCILLER

Christopher Jones is an artist who has worked for DC Comics, Image, Malibu, Caliber, and Sundragon Comics.

TERRY BEATTY INKER

Terry Beatty has inked THE BATMAN STRIKES! and BATMAN: THE BRAVE AND THE BOLD as well as several other DC Comics graphic novels.

GLOSSARY

astounding   causing a feeling of great surprise or wonder

belfry   a tower where a bell hangs. Bats are often seen in belfries.

bleak   not warm, friendly, cheerful, or hopeful

carnival   a form of entertainment that travels to different places that has rides and games

dedicated   having very strong support for or loyalty to a person, group, or cause

dramatic   sudden and extreme

dummy   a doll that is shaped like a person that is used as a puppet

racket   a criminal scheme or activity intended to trick people out of their money

slack   lacking the expected or desired activity

vigilante   a person who is not a police officer but who tries to catch and punish criminals

VISUAL QUESTIONS & PROMPTS

1. Why do you think half of Batman's face is visible here? Why does Batman say he knows how Wesker feels?

2. In this panel, the red sound effect is overlapped by part of the art [the door]. The yellow sound effects, on the other hand, overlap the art. Why do you think this is the case?

3. Why do you think Scarface chose to create an explosive puppet in his attempt to defeat Batman?

4. Scarface has a scar over one eye. Write a short story about how the puppet got its scar.

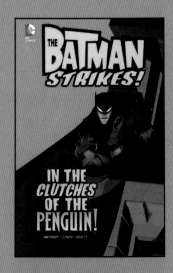

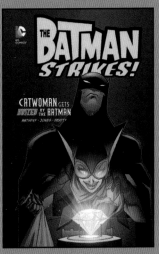